Italy

Italy

Carol Wright

octopus

Contents

First published in 1981 by Octopus Books Ltd
59 Grosvenor Street, London W1

© 1981 Hennerwood Publications Limited

ISBN 0 7064 1534 5

Produced by Mandarin Publishers Limited
22a Westlands Road
Quarry Bay, Hong Kong

Printed in Hong Kong

Endpapers: The five domes of St Mark's Cathedral, Venice
(Photo: David Allen)

Introduction   6

The Flourishing North   8

The Timeless South   20

The People of Italy   30

Italy's Heritage   40

The Spectacular Cities   48

Index   64

Introduction

Italy's incredible wealth of art and architecture has attracted visitors for more than three hundred years. Palaces and cathedrals enfold priceless art collections and not just of the Italian masters. Though one may stumble on a masterpiece in the smallest village church, the three spectacular cities are the largest treasure stores and are a 'must' for a visit. There's Rome with its arches and crumbling pillars as a reminder of former imperial splendour, set against the splashing fountains in little squares; Florence whose artistic endowment extends from the bronze reliefs on the doors of the Baptistry to a tooled leather bag bought on the Ponte Vecchio; and Venice, the unique sea queen, with her foundations washed by polluted water, while her palace roofs still bear the arms of her captains who ruled the sea routes.

The people add to the visitors' sense of being in a country-wide museum: faces that look from a palazzo window recall a Botticelli girl, whilst men with the faces of Magi stand at street corners talking. Italians watch the world go by from a café table, parade for that café society in their best silk scarves and ties, or flash by on a motor bike or in a fast car and sing wherever they can, whether they are waiters or Verdi veterans. Their ebullient enthusiasm is equally apparent whether they are in a football crowd or applauding the local tenor.

The country is diverse. The north has contrasting features: the Alpine wall presenting fine opportunities for skiing; the lakes sealed into semi-tropical hot-houses by more mountains; big industrial plains; extensive, flat sandy beaches and proud old cities with medieval tower houses. The south, the poor relation, overrun by outsiders for centuries, still retains a raw, primitive atmosphere with a life that remains close to the land and to ancient superstitions.

Then having feasted the eyes, one can nurture the body with pasta or pizza and wine in a simple, family-run trattoria or picnic off salami and peaches in some Tuscan field, spiked with cypress trees, or laze on a sunny beach.

Page 1 Fresh market produce sold with a personal touch.
Pages 2 and 3 Venice: the romantic lagoon city.
Pages 4 and 5 The intricate architecture of Pisa cathedral is repeated in the famous Leaning Tower.
Below Tuscany, whose fertile farmland and graceful hills radiate tranquillity.

The Flourishing North

The north is the area of big cities. The Alps form the country's northern wall with ski resorts like Aosta, Sestriere, Sauze d'Oulx and Cortina d'Ampezzo. Within the lower hills are the lovely, secluded Italian lakes.

Most of Italy's agricultural produce is grown on the plain across which the Po river flows and 80% of her manufactured goods are made in this northern triangle. Genoa is a leading port, whilst ships are built at La Spezia and Leghorn. Bologna, once the first university city in Europe, is now important for its food and shoe industry. To the east of this plain, the verdant marshland of Veneto backing Venice is the setting for fine Palladian villas.

Bordering the west coast, Tuscany has Florence as its queen of cities and is loved for its mountainous countryside and wealth of architecture in places like Siena, Pisa and Lucca. Tuscany has massive beach resorts like Viareggio, whilst on the east coast, the Marches region contains the extensive beaches at Rimini. South of Tuscany are the wooded mountains of inland Umbria with centres like Perugia, Assisi and Spoleto and the vineyards of Orvieto. Latium, to the south-west, embraces Rome and the surrounding Castelli area, whilst to the south-east lies the beautiful countryside and coast of the Abruzzi.

The Valle d'Aosta has a French sounding name and, in fact, most people here speak French, though there are also some German-speaking valleys and the valleys in 1947 became an autonomous region. The Aosta valley, or rather the complex of interlinked valleys, runs 120 kilometres (75 miles) along the river Dora Baltea from **Pont St Martin** (previous page) to Courmayeur, the well-known ski resort. Its strategic importance over the centuries has been that it is the junction of the Great and Little St Bernard passes and guards trade routes to the north. In 218 B.C. Hannibal took his army and elephants through the Aosta valley and over the Little St Bernard pass. It is the north face of Italy against the Alps; the valley being overshadowed by the great peaks of Mont Blanc, Monte Rosa and the Matterhorn. The mountains form a natural border wall and glaciers cover 500 square kilometres (200 square miles) of mountain in this area.

The Romans made a road here to take traffic through the mountains to France and Switzerland and their bridge at Pont St Martin marks the beginning of the valley. Aosta was created in 25 B.C. as a Roman outpost in the Alps and named after the Emperor Augustus. Though Aosta is now a modern industrial centre for the production of iron and steel, it has Roman walls and a first century arch of Augustus, erected to commemorate the defeat by Varro of the Salassians, the former valley people. There are also remains of a Roman amphitheatre and a recently excavated forum. St Anselm, an early archbishop of Canterbury, was born in Aosta and there are several city churches dating from 12th to 15th centuries.

In the valley are spas, health resorts, skiing and walking centres. Courmayeur at the north end of Italy, is one of the country's oldest mountain resorts at the foot of Mont Blanc. Cable cars lead up to the Col du Geant at 3,350 metres (11,000 feet). The logical access to the valley is from Turin and Milan or from France through the Mont Blanc tunnel.

The Italian lakes were very popular with 19th century travellers who particularly admired the scenery with its play of light reflected off waters among campaniles, cypresses, orange groves and palms against the backdrop of the Alps. Inseparably linked with the lakes are the **Dolomites** (right), the most poetic and dramatic mountains out of Italy's many ranges.

The lakes, sheltered by their mountains facing the sun, have long been ideal holiday spots. They consist of Lugano and Maggiore partly in Switzerland and Como, the centre of the Italian silk industry, which once had superb lakeside villas like Carlotta, d'Este and Serbelloni, the last two now hotels.

The tranquillity of Lake Maggiore, 3 kilometres (2 miles) wide on the borders of Piedmont and Lombardy, can be experienced by taking a boat from the little resort of Baveno to the Borromean islands. These were named after Carlo Borromeo, archbishop of Milan, whose tomb can be seen in Milan cathedral. On **Isola Bella**, a descendant, Vitaliano Borromeo, built a 17th century villa and splendid gardens (below).

The gardens typify the formality of Italian layouts, descending in ten terraces, with walks and grottoes lined with shells, mirror pieces or marble. Renaissance statues are set among magnolias, camellias, oranges and lemons, spiked with mournful cypress and plumed with palms.

Also in the Borromean islands are Isola Madre, with a botanical garden and palace housing the Borromeo art collection and the Fishermen's island, tiny but with a mini town of churches, cafés, hotels and shops popular with painters and writers.

Lake Garda to the east, with Sirmione, where the Roman poet Catullus was born, is calm and sheltered by high hills giving it semi-tropical vegetation and beautiful gardens. One of the most beautiful lakeside gardens is on the shores of Lake Maggiore, the Villa Taranto, which was created by a Scotsman and covers 40 hectares (100 acres).

The lakes all have plentiful sailing facilities, and boat services using traditional high-backed lake boats, with a central back oar and curved canopies in summer. This is the best way to explore, leaving the cramped lakeside roads which, whilst being a tribute to the national genius for road-building inherent since the Romans, are choked with traffic, twisting round the mountain ledges, and are hot and noisy.

The Dolomites were said to be the first part of the Alps to be freed from ice. The range takes its name from the hard dolomite rock, which is engrained with soft calcite,

eroded by the wind and rain of centuries and sculpted into jagged pinnacles, towers, chimneys, needles, fairy castles, thrones and figures giving rise to plenty of local legends. There are the witches' rock, five towers peaks, the King of Cadore, and the Sausage, a 15-metre (50-foot) tower near the Pordoi pass used to train climbers. The highest and most famous peaks are in the Eastern Dolomites and the true Dolomites are between the river valleys of the Adige and Piave, some eighty kilometres (fifty miles) from west to east.

The best known mountain is Cristallo near Lake Misurina.

This is the Glass Mountain with its local love stories of humble shepherd boy and princess, which inspired a well-known musical piece written for the film named after the mountain.

The Dolomites form a fortress wall between Italy and Austria well crossed by roads and studded with year-round resorts; for example, skiing in summer is possible at Solda. Other popular pursuits are fishing for trout, pike and perch and walking. In spring flowers abound from species so adapted to the cold and height that their seeds must be frozen before they will germinate. Bolzano, guarding the route south over the Brenner pass has a May festival with flower shows and displays of local costumes, customs and crafts. Nearby villages afford splendid mountain views.

Cortina d'Ampezzo is a top skiing resort and was the site of the 1956 winter Olympics. Since Merano is sheltered, it has mild winter temperatures yet is within easy reach of high level skiing. It is famous for its spa qualities gained from the waters, which have a remarkably high radioactive content, soothing digestive and skin diseases. The 4th century B.C. Romans already knew of the special characteristics of Merano and took the 'grape cure', the richness of the grapes being attributed to the radioactive soil. The wines Termeno, Merlano and Rametz are a pleasant medicine indeed.

Spas may have been one early lure for European travellers, but at the beginning of the 20th century, the yachting set formed another chic holiday fraternity. The British moved their base from the Lido at Venice, which was getting too popular, to Rapallo and the Portofino peninsula. The area, while dramatic with high cliffs and varicoloured waters, lacks beaches but has deep, narrow harbours, like **Portofino** (left), ideal for small boats. Camogli, nearby, had a fishing fleet a thousand strong in 1870. Now only a handful of boats rock at anchor below colour-faded houses, hung with washing, and the hotel which was once the home of Genoa's doge. It has a small, attractive beach.

Santa Margherita, where orange trees and the huge, white puff balls of the margherita shrub blossom abundantly, has a beautiful bay and marina. Rapallo has no beach but is a haven for international yachts. At Chiavari chairs, lace and Arab-fringed cotton towels are made. San Fruttuoso is a spot with a diminutive beach and fortress inn reached either by boat or along the cliff top from Portofino, and Paraggi on the car-choked peninsula, flanked by cliffs, is the only sandy beach. Its limpid emerald waters are backed by little restaurants.

Portofino can be viewed either from yachts in the long, narrow bay looking up to the fortified cliffs or down from cliff walks. Cars are thankfully banned from the port side which has a little square of fish restaurants and smart boutiques, from which stairways lead to San Giorgio's church, where the bones of Britain's patron saint are buried. They are carried in procession every April 23. From the lighthouse above the town one can see the whole coastal sweep to La Spezia, Italy's ship-building area.

However, not all Italian weather is suitable for sitting and sipping in little sunlit squares. The northern cities are prepared for inclement weather, yet indulge in the national love of watching the world go by from a café seat. Bologna has its extensive medieval stone arcades, big enough for a horse and rider to cross the city unspotted by rain. In Milan (and southern Naples) there are huge, arched,

glass-roofed galleria (above) which have inspired many a transatlantic shopping mall design.

Milan, the banking, commercial and industrial capital of Italy and centre of the northern region, often shows its civic pride in size. The Gothic cathedral was begun in 1386 but not finished till 1897. It is the world's third largest church and largest Gothic edifice. Its interior where people meet beneath high columns, is austere and more of a galleria extension in atmosphere. Its exterior is dismissed by purists as overdone with its pinnacles, 135 marble spires and 2,245 marble statues as well as a gilded madonna. It gives the effect of fretted light stone and visiting the roof is like wandering in a statuary museum.

Across the cathedral square is La Rinascente, the city's largest store and near that the huge, glass-covered Victor Emmanuel gallery connects the cathedral square with the Piazza della Scala. This is Milan's heart and centre of café life. There's Savini's restaurant or the more modest Biffi's café, shops and bookshops: in general a smart place to meet. The Piazza also houses La Scala opera house that made Verdi renowned. Built in 1779 it has 300 seats and has an opera museum. The building was destroyed in World War II but reopened in 1946 with an inaugural performance conducted by Toscanini.

More open air café life can be experienced in Verona in the Piazza Bra, on one side of which are many cafés and restaurant terraces and on the other, the huge **Roman amphitheatre** (bottom right), which dominates the city and where summer opera performances are held.

Verona is a pleasant city set below Mount Lesini on the banks of the fast-moving Adige river, that flows down from the Dolomites. It is an important commercial centre on route links to Milan and Turin and from Venice and central Italy to Germany and Austria.

Though it is famous for its monumental collection and Roman remains, most people remember it as the setting of Shakespeare's *Romeo and Juliet* and *Two Gentlemen of Verona*. The story of the first, of fated lovers caught between the feuding noble families of Capulet and Montague, reflects the constant fighting between leading families in northern cities in the 13th century. The visitor may see the presumed stone coffin of Juliet in the south-east part of Verona in the Via del Pontiere. To touch it, they say, ensures the everlasting devotion of a loved one. Above the burial crypt is a Roman style cloister with a garden of vines and oranges and a corner window where Juliet is supposed to have left letters for Romeo and nearby is the church where they were married.

From this street the Via Pallone leads to the Piazza Bra and the Roman amphitheatre. Built in 100 A.D., the amphitheatre is well preserved, though several times restored. It holds 22,000 and is the third largest extant after the Coliseum in Rome and that at Capua. The circumference consists of 74 arches compared with 80 in Rome (see page 40). The spectators on the uppermost rows get an excellent view of Verona. Goldoni's first successful tragedy *Belisario* was produced here in 1834 and the 1913 production of *Aida* set new standards of operatic splendour.

Bologna is often called 'the red' after her communist mayor and the terracotta stucco on the many palaces and towers. The colour of the buildings gives a year-round impression of warmth, whilst the 69 kilometres (43 miles) of arched loggias and porticoes along the streets throughout the city give shelter from sun or sleet.

At the end of the 10th century there were some 200 towers in Bologna. These were family status symbols, a common swank idea in the north. San Gimignano in Tuscany still has the best collection with 13. Now in Bologna there are two: the graceful, slender 90 metre (300 foot) **Asinelli** (right) and next to it the Garisenda with its 3 metre (11 foot) list. The two form the city's symbol. Less dramatic are the remains of the Alto Bella tower which pushes its foot into Brunetti's, one of the best restaurants in a city acclaimed as the food capital of Italy. It has, after all, given its name to a way of cooking veal cutlets, a sausage and a spaghetti sauce, made with meat and tomato purée.

Bologna is also nicknamed 'la dotta', the learned, after its international university, where Dante and Copernicus studied. The old university, now a public library, can be visited. The world's first lessons in human anatomy took place here and Galvani discovered electric currents while dissecting frogs at this university. Medicine was then an arts subject and taught in opposition to church wishes. You can still see the spy hole through which the church's inquisitor checked that the taboo subjects of the brain and reproductive organs were not discussed during the dissection of condemned criminals' bodies. Carved wooden figures were also used to depict internal organs. There are 250 handwritten books in the library and above the shelves are the coats-of-arms of pupils who came from all over the civilized world to study at Bologna. A bust of Laura Bassi, an 18th century lady lecturer, commemorates an early blue-stocking, so beautiful she had

to teach behind a curtain, so as not to distract her pupils.

Knowledge was taken seriously here. In the 17th century, Cassini the astronomer sat in a high window alcove inside the church of San Petronio across the square in the city heart, watching the sun every day for ten years so that his sundial would be perfect. This church has side chapels with 15th century primitive depictions of heaven and hell with gorilla-like devils. This was another church that set out to be the largest in the world but a pope stopped this challenge to Rome and, unfinished, the church is only seventh largest.

Bologna has many mementoes of the Middle Ages in its make-up, but **San Marino** (below) is a complete medieval hangover in the 20th century. Covering only 60 square kilometres (23 square miles) and perched on a limestone outcrop of the 820 metre (2,700 foot) high Mount Titano overlooking the Rimini coast, it has been a republic since 885. It remains independently so, making its main living out of stamps, coins, film locations, souvenirs and passport stamps, by enticing visitors to chalk up another country covered. Selling titles and honours to the social aspirant is another income source.

San Marino is said to have been founded in the 4th century in Diocletian's time by one Marino, a Christian stone mason from Dalmatia who was fleeing from persecution. He became a hermit there. San Marino has never

expanded, though Napoleon, impressed by the little state's self sufficiency, offered more land but was refused. The population of 1600 is governed by two regent captains, who are elected every six months and ceremoniously installed in the capital, Montefeltro, on April 1 and October 1 each year and a grand council of 60 made up of landowners', nobles', and burghers' representatives. Its industries, apart from tourism, are making paint, cotton yarn and ceramics. There are three castles, a governor's palace, a church and 120 civic guards in old style uniforms. In World War II the neutral state harboured many refugees from Rimini nearby and suffered damage from 243 British bombs, for which compensation was later paid.

Piedmont is one of Italy's foremost wine-producing areas, though wines are produced successfully all over the country and Italy is now Europe's biggest wine producer. Piedmont wines are strong and mature with a hint of the neighbouring French character. The protective alpine background (Piedmont after all means 'foot of the mountain') gives the **Monferrato hills** (below) a hot growing season and a misty, damp autumn.

From these hills come red wines like Barolo and Barbaresco and other popular wines such as Barbera, Dolcetto, Grignolino and Freisa, which are named after their grapes. From the south east of the area comes Cortese, a white wine. Occasionally the place of origin is added, for example, Barbera d'Asti. Asti is the main town in the area and is famous for Italy's sweeter answer to champagne, Asti Spumante, a sparkling white wine. Asti has its own wine fair in September with a recently revived palio horse race and pageant similar to that of Siena. The Monferrato area is bounded in the north by the Po river and Turin and cut in two by the Tanaro river, which links Asti to Alessandria.

Other good northern wines include Lambrusco from near Modena, Sangiovese from the Bologna area, as well as Valpolicella, Bardolino and Soave from Verona. Chianti, possibly the best known Italian wine, is produced in the Florentine hills south of the city. Other well-known wines from still further south include Orvieto, north of Viterbo, Frascati from around Rome, Verdicchio from the Anconan marches and Est Est Est from near Orvieto. The story of this name is said to come from a worldly bishop, who was so concerned about his stomach that when he went travelling, he sent a servant ahead to test the food and wine available and report back to him. In describing one excellent wine he had tasted, the servant was at a loss for words to describe its superiority. Finally he blurted out 'it is, it is, it is'.

Italy possesses 8,600 kilometres (5,345 miles) of coastline and enough beach variety to satisfy both the gregarious and the solitary. The latter will probably head south to the smaller, cliff-cut more secluded strands of Calabria, whilst the northern beaches are more easily accessible.

In the north, the 240 kilometre (150 mile) long Italian riviera stretches from the French border, through Genoa, down to below La Spezia. At the northern end, following the old Roman road, the Via Aurelia, from Italy to France, it is sheltered by the Alps and there are small sand and shingle beaches with resorts renowned for their flowers. There is San Remo with its pop song festival, or Bordighera, a town which supplies the palms used in Rome's Holy Week processions and an early British holiday maker's favourite. Near Ventimiglia are the Hanbury gardens at Capo Mortola, started by Sir Thomas

Hanbury in 1862 and now displaying over 6000 varieties of plants and trees.

Those who like their beaches big can veer south from the cramped coves of the Portofino peninsula to **Moneglia** (above) in Tuscany, or move across country to Emilia Romagna or the Veneto. In Tuscany, easily accessible from Pisa and Lucca are the four resorts covering a twelve-mile, continuous beach: Marina di Massa, Forte dei Marmi, Marina di Pietrasanta and Viareggio, all backed by hotels and linked by boat to the Gulf of La Spezia and the Tuscan islands. On this great sand beach, the drowned body of Shelley was brought ashore and burned. Walks can be made along to Torre del Lago, the house where opera-composer Puccini wrote *La Bohème*, *Tosca* and *Madame Butterfly* and to the memorial museum nearby.

On the east coast there are the popular and well-packaged resorts of Rimini, Riccione and Cattolica, which in summer display a sardine layout of bodies. The beaches here extend from the river Po estuary and the sea is very shallow and safe for small children. They range from 275 to 900 metres (300 to 1000 yards) in width. Rimini itself is divided between the modern disco and café resort and the charming old town, originally Etruscan, situated at the meeting place of two Roman roads, Emilia and Flaminia. It has a Roman arch built in 27 B.C. and a Roman bridge. Its name is more widely known in literary circles for the unhappy 13th century love story of Francesca da Rimini, murdered with her lover by her husband, which Dante described in his *Inferno*.

Just north of Rimini and south of Ravenna is the Rubicon river, once the border of Cisalpine Gaul, a Roman province. By the act of crossing it, Julius Caesar showed that he was coming south to challenge the power of Rome.

Venice itself has its five kilometres (3 miles) of sand on the Lido, backed by hotels and a casino. Forty kilometres (25 miles) from Venice but connected to it by boat and road, Lido di Jesolo is an excellent resort for families. It has 14 kilometres (9 miles) of soft sand with pine trees and hotels on the beach itself.

The Timeless South

The south consists of four mainland provinces – Campania round Naples and the Sorrento coast; Calabria with its mountains and coastal resorts; Basilicata, the smallest with sun-bleached mountains and Apulia in the east with cities like Lecce, Foggia and Bari – and two islands: Sicily and Sardinia. Compared with the north, it is dry, eroded and neglected. It is cut into isolated regions by mountains and has a deeply indented coastline. Calabria remained feudal into this century with absentee landlords, clannish hill communities and dwindling population. Now improved facilities, communications and growing tourism are helping to revive the area. Sardinia, an island with 1300 kilometres (800 miles) of coastline has proud, reserved people, high mountains and beautiful white, sandy beaches. Sicily, too, is vast. It is known for its poverty, Mafia origins and archaeological remains.

The south reflects its many conquerors. For the Greeks the area was Magna Graecia and Naples, Neapolis, was their 'new city'. The Moors ruled and oppressed the south until driven out by the Normans. After this came Spanish and then Bourbon rule, ending in 1860 with the Unification of Italy.

The terrain is poor and hard to work and the volcanoes, Vesuvius, Etna and Stromboli, the last two still very active, have wrought havoc at various periods.

Cefalu (previous page) looks impressive at any time of day or in any weather. It is set on the north coast of Sicily and its name comes from the Greek word 'kephale' meaning 'head', referring to the shape of its backing rock. Built on a rock spur running towards the sea, its defensive position is typical of Sicilian cities, always on the alert for a new onslaught from outside. Phoenicians, Greeks, Romans, Byzantines, Arabs, Normans, and Swabians have all conquered Sicily at various times.

At Cefalu the fishermen's houses cluster and slither together towards the harbour. The town is dominated by its huge Norman cathedral recalling those of northern France. Roger II began the building in 1131 and it took over a century to complete, even after cutting back on its original more lavish designs.

Though impressive enough in its siting, a talent with the Normans, it is the interior that stuns the visitor. It has a lofty columned, triple nave and some of the best 12th century Byzantine style mosaics in Italy. Behind the cathedral, the rock can be climbed to 278 metres (913 feet) for views out to sea towards the Sicilian satellite islands. This Aeolian group includes Lipari, a pleasant resort and wine island; Stromboli, made popular by the Ingrid Bergman–Rossellini film of the same name and famed for its active volcano which candles the night with fire; and Vulcano. This island has a beach of bubbling volcanic mud, which warms the sea water and provides a free spa treatment through its health-giving but highly sulphurous-smelling mud.

Volcanoes play a big part in the life and legend of Southern Italy but **Etna** (below) on Sicily is the most awesome. It is the largest volcano in Europe, measuring 200 kilometres (125 miles) around its base and rising to

a cone some 3,300 metres (10,900 feet) high: the height varies according to the lava build-up. Believed by the Greeks to be the cyclops workshop and forge of Vulcan, its name means 'blaze' in Greek. There have been 135 recorded eruptions mostly in the Christian era. The 1669 eruption destroyed the town of Catania below. Since 1950 Etna has been very active and destructive. It has been called 'hell at high altitude' but tours to its lip are popular. The lava has produced extremely rich soil that can produce five crops a year and nourish the vines from which the powerful local wines are produced, an ideal accompaniment to the fresh fish dishes.

The best place for contemplating wrathful Etna is from the flower and moss-encrusted seats of the Greek theatre in Taormina. In the 3rd century B.C. the Greeks would watch dawn plays whilst the sun was reflected from Etna's snows (which last from October to May and where skiing is possible). The Romans in 3rd century A.D. renovated the theatre and added the brick 'scena' of columns and arches but still didn't ruin the view. The theatre is famed for its acoustics and is used for summer film and music festivals.

Taormina, founded in the 4th century B.C. by Greeks moving up from Naxos, their first Sicilian colony, is a charmer. The little Corso Umberto, the main street runs along a hill ledge and is lined with 15th and 16th century houses. Rising from it are alleyways of steps, where at night the tarantella dancers and pipers burst out of wine bars to continue in the cool night air. Other places of interest are the squat cathedral, the Corvaia palace museum of Sicilian folk art and the ex-monastery Hotel San Domenico, which formed the wartime headquarters of Field Marshal Kesselring, thereby calling down bombs upon the town. At 470 metres (1540 feet) is Castel Mola, the old Greek acropolis, which is good for dizzying sea views, but Taormina at 210 metres (700 feet), connected by cable car to its beaches, remains the best place for volcano viewing.

After Sicily, Sardinia is the biggest of the Mediterranean islands, covering 24,000 square kilometres (9,000 square miles). It lies 240 kilometres (150 miles) off the coast of Italy but considers itself even more strictly separated from the mainland. Over the centuries the Sards, one of the oldest of the Italian races, have suffered successive invasions, as have the people of Sicily and most of southern Italy, but Sardinia has never been completely conquered. In the 12th century Cagliari, the capital in the south of the island, was developed by the Phoenicians as a trading port. In 1708 Cagliari surrendered to the English fleet but in 1720 came under the rule of the Dukes of Savoy, until the 1860s, when Sardinia became part of the general unification of Italy. In 1948 it was granted political autonomy by the Italian government.

Shaped, so legend goes, like God's footprint, the island is little known, despite its superb beaches and lovely hill ridges in the centre. The Aga Khan's smart holiday development of the Costa Smeralda in the north-east has made the world more aware of the existence of Sardinia but this is only a tiny fraction of the island, which is otherwise undeveloped. The agricultural communities are isolated and old customs, including the vendetta, persist. Cagliari has, in fact, been inhabited since neolithic times. Now, reflecting its many masters, it is a cosmopolitan city, hovering in character somewhere between Europe and Africa. Its early remains

include a second century fortress, the ruins of a Roman amphitheatre, hewn from rock overlooking the bay of Angels and the Punic Roman cemeteries. The 18th century cathedral has a Pisan style facade: Pisan invaders were responsible for most of the Romanesque churches in the south of Italy. The church has a baroque interior and the crypt is decorated with 500 Sardinian style flower designs in stone. Other places of interest are the **Beqizzole castle** (previous page), the archaeological museum and two Pisan style towers, the Tower of the Elephant and of San Pancrazio.

Garibaldi, the man who did much to unify Italy in the

19th century, lived out his final years on Caprera, a little island off the north coast of Sardinia. He died there in 1882.

Capri (above) is one of the islands in the Gulf of Naples not thrown up by volcano Vesuvius' activity. It is part of the limestone Apennine chain; a craggy southern spot to be avoided by sufferers from vertigo. It is popularly known as the island of goats because of the shape of its many rock pinnacles. Its small communities are perched on terraced areas right up to Anacapri at the top. This village is linked to Capri, the main town, by buses which are specially shortened so that they can negotiate

the narrow road bends. Once a pirates' stronghold, the British in the 19th century had the idea of turning it into another Gibraltar and built fortifications, until stopped by the French.

Capri is reached by a rather unnerving helicopter ride from Naples airport or by hydrofoil and ferries. The island's hems of sea-tortured rock can be seen from a boat whilst visiting the Blue Grotto, which is best viewed in the early morning light. There are also green, yellow, pink and white grottoes. High up on the island is the villa of Swedish author Axel Munthe, who wrote the *Story of San Michele* describing his love of the place, a love previously felt by the Emperor Tiberius and many other Romans. Tiberius built twelve villas on the island and refused to return to Rome when he was dying. From the Villa Jovis he is said to have got rid of unwanted house guests by heaving them off the rocks.

The grotto settings for pagan rites, the peaks and the reminders of an emperor's playtime scenes give Capri an air of mystery, despite the tourist traffic during the day which jams the little squares with visitors from Naples and the Sorrento coast resorts. At dusk it becomes quieter. Then people go out to eat in the little waterfront cafés of Marina Grande, whose terraced houses are linked by stairways, or they take the 800 steps to the Castle Barbarossa ruin; or they sip the local wines by the restaurant pool of Canzone de Mar once the home of Gracie Fields.

Stone dug from nearby ground or removed from former buildings created many architectural forms in Italy but none as distinctive as the trulli dwellings of Apulia. Their origin is said to be prehistoric. The local stone here splits easily into thin layers called *chiancarelle*, which are then piled on to a square base without mortar and sloped inwards and upwards to a pointed dome. They are whitewashed inside and sometimes interconnected. Others say the shape is a relic of feudal days, when the houses were made like pointed straw huts so that they were easy to demolish when the landlord came round collecting a housing tax.

Whatever their origin, trulli are still built in this agricultural area, though now with a chimney, instead of holes, to let out the smoke. Some have flat roofs or incorporate a grain store. They are scattered round the countryside, at corners of fields for storing implements, and in many villages. The greatest preserved collection is at **Alberobello** (above), which also has a hotel made with typical whitewashed stone and even a cone-topped church, dedicated to St Anthony.

Just as the trulli are simple dwellings made from what was to hand in the poor neglected south, so **Matera** (right) in the little Basilicata forest province used hollowed-out rock to make its dwellings. Although increasingly abandoned today for lack of amenities,

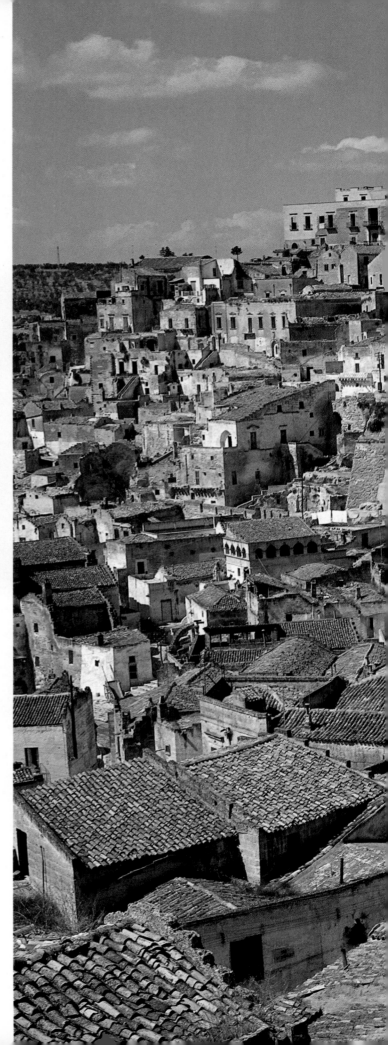

they underline the starkness of life in the provinces in the bottom half of Italy's 'leg'.

Matera is in fact a photogenic beauty, set on a rock escarpment above green fields, olive trees and cypresses. The broad avenue by which it is entered gradually narrows towards the old town, which clings on to hill folds overhanging a cliff. The terraced stone houses seem all walls and windows and have been dug from solid rock, hollowed out, and stacked one above the other up the hill. One can enter a wine shop at street level, then descend one or two levels to drink local wine, thus leaving behind the traffic and the twentieth century. As well as some sixty rock churches dedicated to Saint Basil often niched into crags and difficult to reach, Matera has two main quarters of rock dwellings called sassi, 'the stones', and inhabited since prehistoric times: Sasso Barisano and Sasso Caveoso. But below the 13th century cathedral many of the rock houses are now abandoned.

Many of Italy's southern resorts seem to cling on as tight to the steep stony ground as they do to life. Song-praised **Sorrento** (above) is but one of a chain of resorts clawed into the cliffs, along the Amalfi coast south of Naples and lined by one of the most scenic but stomach-turning roads in a country famous for its great road building.

Outdoor lifts (ascensori) are needed at Sorrento to carry hotel guests to and from the beach but the view is not one of poverty as at Matera. Houses are light and russet-roofed. They are linked by stairs, little squares, hotels and cafés, whilst any gaps between them are filled with citrus trees or flower gardens.

Pagan ceremonies, never far below the surface in southern Italy, were held along this coast in the Baths of Diana caves near Sorrento. The Isles of Mermaids nearby were so named because the coastal grottos were supposed to be the homes of these creatures. Sorrento on the southern tip of the cape separating the Bay of Naples from Salerno bay is a good sailing centre. For a long time Amalfi, 48 kilometres (30 miles) to the south, was an independent maritime power competing with Genoa and Venice. Its former population of 70,000 has now diminished to about 600. Its marine laws codex (still on view in the town hall) governed marine commerce until 1576. Amalfi suffered from crippling tidal waves and in 1343 Petrarch talked of the sea 'devouring Amalfi'.

Among the other Sorrento coast resorts, Ravello was once the residence of the English pope, Adrian IV; and Positano, called 'the poor man's Capri', attracts artists. In spite of mini beaches with black lava, the area is well worth visiting to see its orange and almond trees in blossom at Easter and to view the crafts of coral carving, lace, embroidery and inlaid woodwork. Its life looks out to the blue sea, which at night is studded with fishing boat lamps luring in some of the best fish to be caught in Italy.

The great bay of Naples is a contrast to the land limitations of Sorrento. Guarded by the Castel dell'Ovo on a small island, the city of **Naples** (right) piles up like a great amphitheatre with rows of old and new high-rises, overlooked by castles and topped by hills reached by four funiculars. In the late afternoon the Posillip hill with its umbrella pines symbolic of the south, framing a distant Vesuvius, or the garden belvedere of San Martino monastery at Vomera or the Castel Sant'Elmo are places to sit and see the sun go down into the bay.

Naples, Italy's third largest city, is the seething premier city of the south where baroque gilded and brocaded palaces are contrasted with severe Angevin Gothic churches. Here separate districts even have separate dialects. In the poor Piedigrotta area, alleyways swathed in washing are noisy and prone to epidemics. In Bassi, large families live in single basement rooms of what used to be palaces. This is the Neapolis, the new city of the Greeks, older than Rome. In 3000 years of history it has had eight ruler races and takes architectural ideas from all of them.

Santa Lucia is the waterfront fishing 'village' enshrined in songs sung in the cafés. From the Via Caracciolo which follows the curving sea front, the Piazza Municipio and 13th century Castel Nuovo are near and like Milan, Naples has its Umberto galleria, a cross-shaped glass gallery of covered shops and cafés. Adjacent is the San Carlo opera house built in 1787.

Naples churches compete with their bell tolling and in the cathedral the San Gennaro chapel is a good example of Neapolitan baroque style. There are 13 museums of which the foremost is the National Museum containing artefacts from Pompeii, Herculaneum and Cuma. The Capodimonte museum has a hundred rooms with paintings by the masters as well as the well known porcelain of the same name.

Calabria, for centuries a place of political exile, was so

cut off from Italian national life it has only just been discovered and linked to mainstream life by the Autostrada del Sol which runs from Salerno to Reggio Calabria and by ferry across to Sicily.

Calabria has potential wealth both in its high Sila Mountains and hills which are being reafforested and in its 800 kilometres (500 miles) of beautiful, undeveloped coastline, which is beginning to attract tourists. Hotels are being built but the area still retains many of its old ways and customs. In the hill villages traditional crafts are practised and the villagers speak in dialects brought from other parts of Europe. **Scalea** (left) on the west coast just south of Maratea has modern camp sites near the village. The sun here is tan hot by late May and remains so till almost the end of October. Little resorts near Scalea include Praia a Mare in a river estuary and offshore Isola di Dino, where Ulysses was supposed to have landed. After Scalea comes Cirella with its big straight beach. The hilly Vecchia Cirella, now in ruins, was partly destroyed by Hannibal and much later by Napoleon. This strategic site is found up herb-scented paths by clambering through arches into castle courts, crypts of churches and halls of houses, empty and left for history. From broken turrets, the view way below is of an indigo sea. Diamante, the next fishing port, is named after the translucence of the light reflected off its waters.

The People of Italy

Italians are noisy, volatile and gregarious: they love café life, parading the streets in family finery, cinema, high-powered sports cars and buzzing motorscooters. Amorous bottom pinching and body nudging in crowded buses is a national sport, yet the men are fiercely protective of family honour and adore their children. Italians are beautiful and elegant. Their flair for clothes has made Florence and Rome influential couture centres with designers like Emilio Pucci revered world-wide. Always artistic, even bags and luggage have been elevated to status symbols by Gucci and Magli shoes are among the world's most fashionable. The young men and girls are dark-eyed and shapely, although pasta intake, not to mention the other national inventions of pizza and icecream, sometimes produce more ample figures in men and women.

Menu language may be French, but music's tongue is Italian. The lilting mellifluous sounds can be Romeo's soft, *amoroso* murmurings, rising through *con brio* to Mussolini's *furioso* or to *agitato* when a sleek Lancia or Alfa Romeo has been scraped by someone's Vespa. Speech alone, however, is not sufficient for ebullient Italians' expression. Extravagant hand and body gestures are added, whether by men chatting on street corners, by gondoliers poling down the Grand Canal or waiters serving spaghetti at a Naples waterfront restaurant.

The Italians are a gregarious people, who love to sit and watch passers-by, particularly when they themselves are eating at an **outdoor restaurant** (previous page). Italian food was Europe's first refined cuisine; the Romans perfected the art of elegant, even extravagant feasting and the great Renaissance families kept it alive.

Craftsmanship in gold, silver and leather has also always been a prerogative of Italy, particularly in cities like Florence, where leather and silver schools still exist. Italian shoes are highly esteemed in international circles, with names like Magli being among the most prestigious. The modern needs of the jet set are now chiefly catered for by the designs of **Gucci** (top right) in leather goods, travelling bags, accessories and complementary scarves and clothes; they are coveted and copied all over the world.

Though Italians keep alive the great crafts of the past, they have taken a full part in 20th century technological developments, where their design flair has been coupled with modern materials. The furniture of Casina in Milan and the Magistretti chair are examples of household art; whilst Olivetti typewriters bring style and efficiency to the office world.

The Romans excelled at building roads and setting up communications throughout their Empire; their descendants are still good at transport. They say Mussolini made the trains run on time. Italian railway stations are splendid examples of modern architectural styles and contain many facilities welcome to the traveller, like *alberghi diurni* (day hotels), where one may take a bath or shower and generally freshen up. The Sette Bello train that leaves Milan for Rome in the evening is one of the world's most glamorous means of rail transport. It has a sleek, bullet-like appearance, being one of the earliest streamlined trains.

As is loudly apparent in any street in any town in Italy, the Italians love speed and noise. The speedway scream of traffic made up of Vespas weaving in and out, two-tone horns and machismo manoeuvres prove this, though liberated ladies now also have taken to **driving motorbikes** (above) or can be seen precariously riding pillion with their skirts awhirl. Fiat produce family cars from the motor industry centre of Turin and it was an Italian, Issigonis, who put the engine design in Leyland's Mini. Italian cars are popular in many other countries, with Ferrari and Lamborghini being prized as status symbols. The world's racing tracks reverberate to the high performance pedigree names like Alpha Romeo and Lancia, that dashing young (and older) men love to own. The Italian Grand Prix is held at Monza near Milan every September.

Shopping in little neighbourhood stores (below) which provide the freshest of foods is still a pleasure for Italian women who, outside the major cities, have not yet quite succumbed to supermarkets. There are about 3¼ million cows and 7 million sheep, goats and water buffalo in Italy. And while the Italian is not too keen on the 'drinka pinta' idea, half the milk of those animals goes into cheese. The granite-hard parmesan, made in huge wheels and grated finely to sprinkle on pasta and the semi-soft provolone, often sold fashioned into animal shapes in Bologna, are at least a thousand years old; others like Bel Paese, a mere half century in age or origin. Pecorino Romano is made from fresh sheep's milk; gorgonzola is a rich, creamy, blue-veined cheese, ricotta is a type of cottage cheese and mozzarella is made from water buffalo milk in the south. Fresh and dripping with buttermilk, this is prized by the housewives of Naples, who use it in pizzas or to make the delightful savoury, *mozzarella in carrozza* ('cheese in a carriage'), a cheese sandwich dipped in flour and beaten egg and fried. The pear-shaped provolone that hangs in shops is a version of caciocavallo, so-called because it is strung in pairs

as if to be carried home across the pommel of a mule. Butirri caciocavallo has an egg-sized piece of butter inside, so that when it is sliced across the two flavours can be enjoyed together.

Markets too are a joy in Italy, demonstrating the Italians' liking for fresh foods, their love of meeting together and talking and also their sense of drama when buying from stallholders. In Venice, the fish and vegetable markets have served the public for over a thousand years. In Genoa and Naples the Sunday markets are important social occasions when everyone goes there after church, dressed in his best. In Rome, there is a Sunday Flea market and at Crotone, in Pythagorus square in the very heel of Italy, one of the most traditional of European markets still persists.

Fish is particularly rich from the bay of **Naples** (left) and popular seafoods with Italians are tuna (served with veal in *vitello tonnato*), red mullet, scampi and fritto misto, a crispy mix of deep-fried seafood pieces including octopus tentacles. Sardines are much eaten in Sicily and Sardinia and in the south the old ways of catching fish are still practised; for example, in Calabria shark are harpooned from a cliff top or high prowed boat in the same way that Homer described it. **Pizza** (right) is the great take-out treat of Italy, particularly in Naples and the little coastal resorts of the Sorrento coast, where pizza restaurants are strung along the road. And the idea has spread to many other countries. It's so loved in the States, it has become an established part of the American way of eating. On top of the dough, tomato purée is spread, then comes soft cheese, a scattering of herbs, an anchovy or two, or perhaps sliced mushrooms, black olives as a garnish and a sprinkling of oil to make the crust shiny. Then it is baked in ovens that are often on show either in the open air or at the back of restaurants.

Italian food is not all pasta, pizza and icecream, though these dishes have been successfully exported world-wide. There is a rich variety in the dishes which make ample use of meats, fine smoked Parma hams, fresh vegetables, herbs and the excellent fish. Bologna is the food capital of the north and the cookery there is based on wealth. An exotic delight here are the white truffles handed freely in autumn to restaurant diners to grate over their pasta. Naples dominates the southern cuisine, which is based on a more poverty-influenced cookery and makes use of whatever is to hand. Here the visitor can enjoy eating out at the waterfront fish restaurants of Santa Lucia listening to singers and waiters. This incidentally is another widespread Italian export; in New York, for example, at Asti's waiters combine singing and serving. Other notable dining-out spots are the courtyards of ancient buildings in Rome's Trastevere, the canal sides or St Mark's Square in Venice, terraces in Taormina, the Piazza della Signoria in Florence or along Rome's Via Veneto, *the* place to be seen and be snapped by the itinerant photographers for the press and to ogle at the ladies of the night who parade here. There is an enormous variety of Italian drinks to choose from, including Campari Sodas (ready mixed here), Martinis, Cinzano, Galliano, Strega and Sambuca (which is flamed with a coffee bean). The Italian may start his day for convenience and swiftness with a stand-up *espresso* (black coffee) and roll in a café, but later in the day he likes to relax with a *cappuccino* (frothy white) and perhaps a grappa, an Italian brandy.

Italy adores its old customs and costumes and loves an excuse to dress up. The 700 year-old traditional Venetian gondola regattas in September use patrician gondolas for the **parades and races** (next page). This is but one example of the many parades, processions and gala occasions that can be seen in Italy. Others include Siena's horse race, the palio; Florence's medieval football game; the gigantic procession at Messina in which 9 metre (30 foot) high monster figures on horseback commemorate the beginning of the city; and Bologna has its children's carnival. Many of the processions and parades have a religious significance or are associated with witchcraft and primitive beliefs. Epiphany masses in some areas have priests with swords and helmets as a reminder of ruler soldier priests of the past. In the south, Easter is often celebrated with ferocity and realism; at Cosenza in Calabria, for instance, 180 kilogramme (400 lb) statues of wooden saints are paraded for up to five hours; and at Taranto a fish supper is served on the waterfront, while hooded penitents sway trance-like to funeral marches played by the town bands. In the hill villages of Calabria in Holy Week, the Vattienti or scourgers use whips with glass or pin-ended thongs, and a funeral in Calabria with the strange repitu chants has more of the savage feeling of a Greek tragedy about it.

Italians all have a close affinity with music and in fact their language is used throughout the world to express musical terms and instruments, such as *sonata, concerto, allegro, andante, presto,*

piano forte, *viola* and *cello*. Violins were produced in Cremona in the Middle Ages by such masters as Stradivarius, Guarnieri and Amati. And Italian composers are world-renowned from Palestrina, Vivaldi and Monteverdi, through to Donizetti, Verdi, Puccini and Rossini. Toscanini (1867–1957) was a world-famous conductor and the tradition is continued with Abbado.

Italians love to see their life styles reflected in drama and the success of neo-realism in the Italian cinema underlines this. A passion for cinema to equal that for football matches exists throughout Italy and the country has produced many leading directors of recent years: Vittorio de Sica, Roberto Rossellini, Dino de Laurentis, Visconti, Mastroianni, Fellini with his *La Dolce Vita*; Bertolucci and Michelangelo Antonioni. Though Italian men have the reputation for lusty Latin loving, a penchant for pressing and patting women in public and make jealous husbands and doting fathers (to kill your wife's lover is not considered a crime in Sicily), the screen is dominated by beautiful, enduring women with not least of their charms the ample spaghetti busts. Sophia Loren, Anna Magnani, Sylvana Mangano, Claudia Cardinale, Gina Lollobrigida and Monica Vitti have all become internationally well-known.

La Dolce Vita for many includes possessing a status symbol from one of the top Italian designers. The Italian collections rate highly on the international scene and Emilio Pucci is one of the best known of designers using silk in sizzling colours to make his impact. Ferragamo is a leading shoe designer and has more recently gained a reputation for his garments, whilst Roberta di Camamino is another prestigious name in clothes design. Florence and other important cities are full of elegant boutiques presenting these and similarly well-known couturiers' clothes in arresting window displays which are an art form in themselves. The Italian silk industry, centred at Como on Lake Garda, is at the forefront of European fashion, building its reputation with subtle blends of colours for both heavyweights and light chiffons. Expert use of colour and line is seen in many items, even the humble moulded plastics at which Italy excels.

Though industry in the north of Italy accounts for a large proportion of the workforce, over fifteen million Italians all over the country earn their living by **agricultural work** in which the whole family often join (right). In the south, the three most common Mediterranean crops – wheat, vines and olives – are extensively grown, sheep are kept and a large amount of land is given over to citrus trees. Tomato growing also provides work for many, especially at **harvest time** (below). When the yellow tomato first appeared in Europe, brought from the New World, it was named pomodoro (golden apple) by the Italians. Then, in the late 16th and 17th centuries, they developed new, larger, red varieties. Now the rich colour and piquant flavour of southern Italian tomatoes have found world export markets, either canned or in purée form and these are ideal to make the sauces that flavour pizza and pasta. In the south, bunches of tomatoes are strung up on house walls to dry so that they can be eaten through the winter till the next crop is ready.

In the north, the rich, central Po valley produces most of the crops and supports a large proportion of the cattle kept. Below the Po plain, Tuscany, though it contains a wide variety of crops, is characterized by vines and cypresses, which give it a tranquil beauty much loved by visitors.

Italy's Heritage

Italy is a country-sized art collection reflecting many centuries of talent in its antiquities, its paintings, its sculptures and its churches.

Great architecture was brought to Italy by the Greeks in the fifth century B.C., when they settled in Sicily and southern Italy. The remains at Agrigento, Selinunte, Segesta and Paestum are witness to this. However, evidence of an earlier civilization exists in the ancient nuraghe buildings of Sardinia. The Romans, from the 8th century B.C. to the 5th century A.D., added colour with their lively mosaics, as can be seen from the excavated works at Pompeii and Herculaneum.

Mosaics were also used in church decoration in the Middle Ages, when the Byzantine tradition dominated Italian art. The style, preserved in the superb Ravenna church mosaics, was without three-dimensional effects and lacked realism. Early churches and their treasures acted as the artistic link between the great days of the Pax Romana when Rome ruled the world and the Middle Ages after the expulsion of Byzantium, during which period Europe went into its justly termed 'dark ages'.

Cimabue and Giotto introduced a more realistic style as can be seen from their work at Assisi. Sculptors of the great Florence school, like Donatello continued the trend towards realism, culminating in the outstanding works of the Renaissance.

In Rome the **Flavian amphitheatre** (previous page), the Coliseum's original name, shows the ruthless, bloodthirsty side of imperial Rome. Built from 72–80 A.D. on the orders of Vespasian on the site of Nero's Golden House, the 48 metre (159 foot) high arena with its 550 metre (1,800 foot) circumference extends above a warren of cages, corridors and cells. The stones were put in place by 20,000 slaves and prisoners, many of them Hebrew. Eighty arched passages called *vomitoria* let in crowds to see the day-long spectacles of wild beast struggles, gladiatorial combats and, when flooded, naval combats.

Christians met their deaths here too. The presence of wild animals brought from all over the then-known world was confirmed by over 400 species of plants, which had grown up from the seeds they brought in their bodies, and which were still flourishing when the coliseum was excavated in 1875. Honorius forbade gladiatorial fights in 405 and the coliseum eventually became a 13th century fortress and stone quarry for Renaissance palaces until declared a sacred place by Pope Benedict XIV in 1750 as a memorial to martyred Christians.

Before the glory that was Rome, the Greeks ruled in the Southern Italian colony, which they called Magna Graecia. One of their greatest and less visited remains is Paestum, 50 kilometres (31 miles) from Salerno. Built as Poseidonia in 600 B.C. and renamed in 173 when the Romans took over, Paestum has been protected from the curious and stone-stealing builders by the fact that it is sited on marshes which harboured malaria till relatively recently. The sea has now receded across these marshes but the great temple of Neptune still stands, along with the remains of two other 6th century B.C. Doric temples, to **Ceres** (below), the goddess of fertility and crops and to Poseidon. The time to see these temples is at sunset, as the dying light gilds the fluted columns. These columns are severely classical in

their symmetry and later served as an inspiration to
Bernini, the famous architect, sculptor and painter.

A more entrancing view of the home life of the Roman
empire is seen at **Pompeii** (above) and at the less well-
known Herculaneum; one a Roman pleasure resort, the other a
spa south of Naples, both engulfed in 79 A.D. by the
eruption of Vesuvius. The two died differently: Pompeii
with a hail of small red hot stones, Herculaneum by a
slow thick sealing flow of lava mud. For this reason it
has been easier to excavate Pompeii to reveal complete
street patterns. The mosaic floors and wall frescoes
also unveiled show Pompeiian red, a shade never
successfully imitated by modern painters. After nearly
2,000 years, the colours are still bright and the satyrs,
nymphs and maidens dance or recline languidly; some scenes
are naughty, others simply idyllic. Pompeii shows how richly
Rome lived and how elegantly they placed art on the floor
and walls of their dwellings; an art that continued
as part of the Italian heritage. Caught in disaster
too are the simple, normally perishable things of life:
some loaves, the lunch set out for a priest, mulled
wine in a shop, a necklace dropped in the panic.

Even older are the **nuraghe buildings of Sardinia** (left).
These megalithic, cone-shaped constructions are built of
huge stones piled dry on one another. The nuraghese were
ancient Sardinian warriors known for attacking enemies
with stone balls. About 7,000 nuraghe buildings exist on
the island, sited on hill tops commanding sweeping views

or tucked away in wooded surroundings. Shepherds today imitate their structure but there is a difference of opinion as to the dating and purpose of the original buildings. A whole nuraghe village with towers, galleries and armouries at Barumuni is said to date back to the 11th century B.C. The sturdy structures rising to 18 metres (60 feet) with walls up to 7 metres (23 feet) thick, in which whole communities and their animals could be protected, must have been some form of fortress or sanctuary in harsh primitive times.

Leonardo da Vinci (1452–1519) was the all-round genius of the Renaissance. He was a painter of, for instance, the **Last Supper** (below), architect (of the Sforza castle in Milan), town planner and engineer, as much concerned with man learning to fly as with painting the wings of an angel. 'To see is to know' was his philosophy, using his talents as an artist to reveal science to mankind. Nowadays scientists write a report about a discovery; Leonardo drew it. The Palazzo dell' Ambrosiana in Milan has 1,750 of his drawings and Vinci, his birthplace on the slopes of Monte Albano, has a collection of machines made from his models in its 13th century castle. He developed the camera obscura, reflecting a picture on the back wall of a box and did

a sketch for a flying machine in which the pilot moves four wings with pulleys, constituting the first rational approach to the dreams of Icarus. He was also the first to make exact pictures of the human body as sketches of the child in the womb in the Royal Library at Windsor show.

After studying under Verocchio at Florence, Leonardo went to Milan to learn science and technology. Here he painted his first masterpiece, the *Last Supper*. With superb ceiling perspective and rich colours, this spreads gracefully and naturally across the wall of the Dominican monks' refectory, alongside the church of Santa Maria delle Grazie. Unfortunately, however, the painting has been damaged by damp, was splintered by bombing in the last war and is in constant need of restoration.

As can be seen at Pompeii, the Romans were masters of the art of floor mosaics. Later on the mosaics were applied to walls and the world's first bikini picture is a mosaic from the 3rd century at the Villa del Casale in Sicily. After 313 when freedom of worship had been granted under the edict of Milan, mosaics were much used in early church decoration.

At the beginning of the 5th century, Ravenna, south of Venice, took over from Rome as the capital of the Roman Empire, first of the western part and then, with

Justinian in 539, of the whole empire. Saints, magi, virgins, white-robed figures on green fields backed with gold, Justinian's empress Theodora with courtiers, all glorify the walls of the **6th century churches** (below). There is Sant' Apollinare in Classe (once the port of Ravenna but long since silted up, where Dante wrote his *Divine Comedy* and died); Sant' Apollinare Nuovo and San Vitale. Exquisite also is the mausoleum of the Roman lady, Galla Placidia. Her body was brought from Rome to rest beneath fifth century mosaics which are lit by diffused light from alabaster windows.

Sandro Botticelli (1445–1510) stands a little apart from his contemporaries with his magical, delicate sense of line and colour. Though a deeply religious man, he painted many pagan subjects like his great **Birth of Venus** (top right). The church disapproved of this cult among painters of the time but to Botticelli Venus was a poetic dream, the rebirth of mankind, the great hope of the Renaissance.

Botticelli painted to the commissions of the Medici in Florence; his fragile, aristocratic figures were set in luxury but always with a touch of wistfulness or melancholy. Now hanging in the Uffizi gallery, the *Birth of Venus* was painted in about 1477 for a Medici cousin and

hung in his villa at Castello. The Venus is grave not lustful, more like a madonna in her quiet sweetness. A more serious side of Botticelli can be seen expressed in the Sistine Chapel frescoes for which, like Michelangelo, Leonardo da Vinci and Raphael, he travelled from Florence to Rome to paint at the pope's request. Botticelli admired Savonarola and, dismayed at his

betrayal and death at Florentine hands, painted *Calumny*, an allegorical work showing the injustice of violence committed by humanity, rich and poor alike.

Leonardo returned to Florence in the year Michelangelo completed his statue of David, a heroic symbol of Florence. Though a rival and different in temperament, Michelangelo was another multi-talented master of the Renaissance (1475–1564); painter, poet, sculptor and architect. But he was not interested in science and saw his artistry as a gift from God to be inspired by him. His uncertain temper varied from hope to despair and he seems to have been the archetypal image of genius. The brooding power is seen in his figures in the Sistine Chapel ceiling painting, the largest single work by an artist and in the chapel's *Last Judgement* on the altar wall. In the church next door, St Peter's, for which he designed the dome, is his **Pietà** (right) created when he was in his early twenties. It is sweetly tragic: the young, sad madonna, the limp body of her dead son on her knees. It was the only work Michelangelo ever signed: across the madonna's sash. The Pietà was attacked with a hammer in 1972 but has been restored and now resides behind electronic alarms and a shatterproof screen. Michelangelo broke up a much later Pietà himself. This had been

designed for his own tomb but the marble was faulty. A pupil put it together and it can now be seen in Florence cathedral. A third Michelangelo Pietà, the last to be worked on, is in the Sforza castle in Milan.

St Peter's is the world's largest Christian church; comparative sizes of other competitors are marked on the nave floor, in which there is also a porphyry disc where Charlemagne knelt to be crowned Holy Roman Emperor in 800 A.D.

In the 17th and 18th centuries, papal Rome was in an ideal position to commission paintings and sculptures as is demonstrated by the works of many famous artists to be seen in **St Peter's** (left). The high altar under Michelangelo's dome is a simple block of Greek marble from the Forum of Nerva. It is canopied by the 29 metre (95 foot) high bronze baldacchino by Bernini. This is heavily decorated with scrolls, laurels, flowers and figures and supported on barley sugar twist columns, the baroque casting of which was made with bronze from the Roman Pantheon. Only the pope can celebrate mass at this altar before which 89 oil lamps continually burn. In front of the altar is a sunken *confessione* and bronze gates to the tomb of St Peter. In 1940 grottoes beneath the church were opened

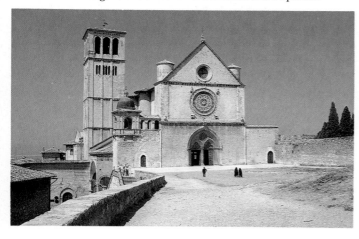

up to show the tombs of the popes. Behind the baldacchino is the wooden and ivory chair of St Peter protected with a Bernini baroque covering. There is also a bronze statue of St Peter dating from the 12th–13th century; the toe of which is worn thin by the kisses of the faithful.

St Francis might well have been an art patron, had he not changed his life style after a spell in a Perugia prison as a result of one of the typical inter-city fights of the time. Born in 1182, the son of a rich cloth merchant, he was brought up to live the good life. Yet he was only in his twenties when he founded his order of mendicant friars and was joined by St Clare, who founded the Poor Clares for women. When he died in 1226, St Francis asked to be buried on a hill where executions had taken place. It was renamed 'Hill of Paradise'. St Francis was canonized in 1228 and **Assisi cathedral** (above) was built over his tomb. The body was so well hidden by his followers that it was not until 1818 that it was discovered two flights below the floor of the church. Four kilometres (two miles) east of Assisi, surrounded by trees, is the Eremo delle Carceri, a hermitage built in the fifteenth century, which was a favourite retreat of St Francis His ascetic life is confirmed both by the collection of personal relics in the sacristy of Assisi church: his goading girdle of camel hair and needles and his crude

sandals and by the roses of the garden of Santa Maria degli Angeli, where he rolled to subdue temptation, since when the roses have been thornless. Yet this asceticism gave rise to a blossoming of rich art, the beginning of Renaissance and indeed modern art in which the human form became depicted in natural shapes and the face of the Virgin was modelled by the artist's wife or even mistress. Cimabue's portrait of St Francis in the lower church of Assisi's two level cathedral is thought of as one of the first naturalistic portraits. Giotto, who 140 years after St Francis' death did much of the work here, is considered the first 'modern' painter. His 28 scenes of the life of St Francis are painted on the lower nave walls. St Francis himself was the first to put replicas of cribs in churches (now such an important part of the Italian Christmas), so that people would be reminded of the humble origins of Christ.

Amalfi cathedral (above) is a surprise; not many smaller seaside resorts have such splendour. Built in the 10th century, rebuilt in the 13th and altered in the 18th century, the cathedral represents a blend of styles of the south: Greek, Moorish, Lombard, Norman and early Gothic. It has a rather sensational multi-coloured façade above a steep flight of steps. The coloured marble is crowned with a mosaic showing Christ enthroned. The bronze doors came from Istanbul and the building reflected the high maritime power of Amalfi in the 10th century. The interior is baroque with an 18th century gold leaf ceiling. The crypt contains the remains of St Andrew also brought back from Istanbul. It is believed a miracle occurs when, on his feast day, his tomb oozes a dark liquid.

The
Spectacular Cities

The special appeal of Rome, Florence and Venice lies in the richness of their historical and cultural associations. Each city has a unique character formed by the part it plays in the life of Italy and by the influence of the people who have lived and worked there.

Rome, the capital of both Italy and the Catholic Church, the Eternal City, has a modern overlay with its cinema city and new high-rise suburbs. Though imperial ghosts dwell in the ancient Roman sites, Christians now come from all over the world to worship at St Peter's.

Florence, because of its position on a trade route, became a centre of banking and insurance. As a result, wealthy families, such as the Medici, both established artists with their patronage and made their homes in magnificent palaces, such as the grand Pitti Palace and the Palazzo Vecchio, whose 100 metre (300 foot) tower is the city symbol.

Venice is a lagoon city, built out of the water, five kilometres (3 miles) from the mainland. It was the most powerful of the Italian republics from the fourteenth to sixteenth centuries. It called itself Serenissima, the most serene, had its own calendar and was ruled by 'doges'. Its many superb buildings are reached by canals which in turn are crossed by numerous bridges. As the poet Browning noted, 'the sea's the street there'. He died overlooking the high street of the Grand Canal alongside of which there are two hundred palaces housing masterpieces by the Venetian school of painters, such as Titian, Tintoretto, Veronese, Tiepolo and Canaletto.

Rome

There is a symphonic poem by Respighi, *The Fountains of Rome*, whose fluting, plangent notes evoke the ubiquitous jets of water – bright and sharp by day and opalescent in their night-time floodlighting – that compensate for much of the traffic trauma and crowd compression in the city's narrow streets.

In the evening, Romans come, through long-established custom, to sit and cool down by a local fountain, most of which mark and honour the source of a city water supply. And at weekends the city-dwellers escape to water gardens like Tivoli and Caserta in the country around the capital. Roman water comes from the Apennine hills and before it was piped to every house, at the beginning of this century, fountain water formed a social gathering point and the tradition lingered on.

The Triton fountain blows an arc of water from a conch shell in the Piazza Barberini at the start of the chic Via Veneto and here also is Bernini's charming little fountain of the bees. The Piazza Navona near the Pantheon opens from narrow streets and contains another of Bernini's fountains: the fountain of the four rivers – Nile, Ganges, Danube and de la Plata – which spurt from beneath an obelisk. This traffic-free square is on the exact site of the first century stadium of Emperor Domitian. Sporting events were later held there and it was often flooded to provide an artificial lake. Now in December, the Befana, a Christmas street fair of market stalls, is held here.

However, Rome's most celebrated waterworks – at least as far as the visitor is concerned – is the **Trevi fountain** (previous page). It inspired the film title *Three Coins in the Fountain* and those who wish to return to the Eternal City must toss in a coin, 'rescued' at

night by local children. The Trevi fountain was ordered by Pope Clement XII and finished in 1762 by Salvi. In the 18th century, there was the legend that those drinking the fountain's pure waters would come back to Rome. The water cascades down the fountain wall, which is backed by the Palazzo Poli with its figures of Neptune being hauled through the waters by sea horses. It comes from a spring 21 kilometres (13 miles) away, which was discovered by a virgin in Roman times and whose waters, along with supplies from other springs, daily provide Rome with twenty million gallons of water, brought to the city by means of an aqueduct, built in 19 B.C. by an Augustan general, Marcus Agrippa.

The Ponte Sant'Angelo leads up to the grim circular bastion of the **Castel Sant'Angelo** (left) which was once the security centre of the distrustful Middle Ages. It was originally built by Hadrian as his imperial mausoleum and succeeding emperors were buried there. Stripped of its splendours and made into a fortress, it played a kindly part in history, when Pope Gregory the Great in 590 saw the vision of an angel sheathing his sword over the castle, predicting the end of a plague. This legend gave the castle its name and the winged statue on top.

Its angelic association stopped there. For many years it became a papal fort; a sanctuary to which popes fled for their earthly safety along an underground passage that connected with the Vatican and which still exists. The popes kept their treasure safe there, in massive chests still on display in the castle. In the last sack of Rome in 1527, Pope Clement VII, besieged but safe in Sant'Angelo, watched helplessly as Germans and Spanish ravaged the city.

The castle became, after the Renaissance and until early this century, a prison with an unhappy record of death and torture. The cells are off a spiral ramp. The castle's terraced battlements from which many prisoners were hanged are celebrated in the final act of Puccini's opera, *Tosca*, when the heroine throws herself to death from them.

Now the rock solid castle, that took six years to build, is a museum containing military relics and Renaissance furnishings. The land around has been made into a park and there are good views of St Peter's Square from the upper terrace.

Rome has many other relaxing gardens and enchanting squares like the Borghese, and Janiculum, or the Villa Sciarra, where one can experience the setting of a private palace garden. The **Spanish Steps** (above) is a place where many tourists go and just sit. In the early 19th century it was the British colony's focal point. Keats' house, where he worked and died, overlooks the steps on the right and Shelley and Byron also worked nearby. It now houses a museum to the Romantic poets and many scholars – the visitors book is a literary who's who – come to study in the library here.

The Spanish embassy to the Holy See in the Piazza di Spagna at the bottom gave the steps their name; otherwise they owe nothing to that country. The money to create the 137 steps came in the eighteenth century from a French ambassador. The broad travertine stone steps lead up to three landings and curve in two sweeps to the front of the Trinita dei Monti church with its twin belfries. This is the major French church in Rome.

In the noisy little Piazza di Spagna is the Barcaccia fountain by Pietro Bernini, the father of a more famous son who designed St Peter's Square. The boat-shaped fountain commemorates the stranding of a river barge when the Tiber flooded long ago. Out of this square runs Rome's famous shopping street, the Via Condotti with its Gucci headquarters and Bulgari's jewellery shop and the old Caffe Greco whose many famous past patrons have included Goethe, Wagner, Chopin, Liszt, Byron and Elizabeth Browning.

However, the greatest of all Rome's squares is undoubtedly **St Peter's** (preceding pages) which, at Easter, becomes the focal point of the Christian world, when 300,000 pilgrims crowd the area. It is subtly sloped up from the church, so all can see the great church's façade and the Pope on his balcony blessing the city and the world.

The square is actually elliptical, measuring at its widest point 226 metres (247 yards), and took Bernini, ''the baroque genius'', ten years to design and twelve years to build from 1655–67. The square is enclosed by two wings with 284 columns in ranks of four and covered with a roof topped with 140 statues of saints. If one stands on either of the two round green marker stones near the central obelisk, the symmetry is perfect and the quadruple flanks of columns become just a single row. The 26 metre (84 foot) high obelisk topped with a cross is the only Roman one not overthrown. It originally marked the goal post of Nero's circus and saw earlier Christians under less happy circumstances. It took 900 men and 140 horses four months to raise it in position. The square has two plain water jet fountains.

The superbly balanced square is but the setting for **St Peter's Church** (inset, preceding page), the largest Christian church in the world and head of the Catholic faith. It covers 1½ hectares (3½ acres) and has 537 steps to its dome. The façade is by Carlo Maderno in Renaissance style with 5½ metre (18 foot) statues on the roof. The central door is a remnant of an older basilica and to its right is the Porta Santa, the Holy Door, only opened in Jubilee Years.

Adjoining the church is the Vatican, the home of the Pope. It is watched over by Swiss guards wearing uniforms said to have been designed by Raphael or Michelangelo, though this theory is strongly denied by some experts, and holding pikes. The church and Vatican are also patrolled by nuns checking on the decency of visitors' clothing and local hawkers rent out plastic raincoats to cover those too scantily clad before they enter the sanctified places.

The riches of the Vatican museum are staggering and are housed in over a thousand rooms and corridors. There are 460 paintings by great masters in 15 rooms; several museums of antiquities; and the Vatican library which is so big, it has never been fully catalogued. The collection is protected by the latest electronic security devices. But the most prized spot is the Sistine Chapel, named after Sixtus IV, who ordered it, with its frescoes by Botticelli, Ghirlandaio and Rosselli and spectacular ceiling that took Michelangelo four years to paint, lying on his back with paint dripping in his eyes. It is still the pope's chapel and the place where the cardinals assemble to elect a new pope. The little stove in this room sends up black smoke if no pope is chosen and white when a new incumbent of the throne of St Peter is elected, to the joy of the waiting crowds in the square.

Florence

The Piazza Duomo, the cathedral square, is the heart of Florence. It contains the **cathedral** (below), the Giotto bell tower (also in the picture), which is 88 metres (290 feet) high and begun in 1434, the baptistry of St John the Baptist (the patron saint of the city) and the cathedral of Santa Maria del Fiore. Lions, also a city symbol, were once kept in cages in the square.

The baptistry, originally built in 1000, was the city's first cathedral and is famed for Donatello's wooden statue of Mary Magdalen and the Byzantine mosaics inside and outside for the bronze doors by Andrea Pisano and Ghiberti set into the octagonal green and white marble façade. The eastern entrance, finished after 1425 is made up of ten panels of old testament scenes and was described by Michelangelo as fit to be the gate of paradise, but was unfortunately dented by the 1966 floods.

Florence's wealth derived from wool processed in the monasteries. As in England, much wool wealth went into beautifying the churches. A fabulous amount of time as

well as money was invested in the cathedral. It took 150 years to build and was designed to be the largest church in the world, which it was when consecrated in 1436. The interior is severe and sparingly decorated. The exterior is better known; the great dome, designed by Brunelleschi and finished in 1461, dominates Florence's skyline and the 463 steps to its 91 metre (300 foot) high top can be climbed for the views. Red, white, and green 19th century marble faces the exterior. Often overlooked, however, is the cathedral museum just behind it, which contains works of art originally created for the church, including choir stalls by Donatello and Della Robbia and a silver altar to St John made by ten top Florentine craftsmen and taking 100 years to complete.

Florence's title of world art capital from 14th–16th centuries is reflected in the many art collections both inside in museums, like the **Pitti Palace** (top right) and outside, notably in the **Piazza della Signoria** (bottom right). The Pitti Palace is the largest and proudest of all palaces. In 1440 Luca Pitti asked Brunelleschi to design a palace

more imposing than anything the Medici owned. Unfortunately Pitti was soon disgraced and his palace sold to the Medici in 1549. Until the 18th century, the Medici family added to it till it was 83 metres (272 feet) long and 36 metres (118 feet) high and covered 97,000 square metres (104,000 square feet). In 1919 it was presented to the state by King Victor Emmanuel III.

The Palatine gallery, though damaged in the 1966 floods, has about 500 paintings, hung on silk-lined walls in an arrangement originally designed to please the nobles of the 17th century. The rooms are named after the subject of the ceiling painting and contain works by many world famous Renaissance artists; there is also a gallery of modern art and a museum of silverware.

The Pitti was built on rising ground. Alongside are the Boboli gardens. These are used in May for concerts as part of the Florence Arts Festival and show the formality of Italian classical gardening. From the terraces of the gardens are good views of the city and the cathedral's dome, which many painters have depicted.

Coming into the Piazza della Signoria at night with its white floodlights on a copy of Michelangelo's statue of David, its darkened arches and the talk and music of its cafés set against the rather severe stones of the Palazzo Vecchio, is like walking into a historical stage set. The city's largest square and the focal point for election speeches, it was once filled with the tower houses of the Uberti family. After their defeat in one of the endless noble bickerings during which the buildings were razed to the ground, houses were banned from the site.

In the 15th century Florence was a free republic commune ruled by trade guilds and two councils. For three centuries, the Medicis ruled and built. The Palazzo Vecchio was built as a centre of government and for defence. It was later used as the chamber of deputies' hall when Florence was Italy's capital under united Italy. Many of its art-filled rooms are open to the public. The apartments of the Medicis, who slept in gilded beds under golden damask curtains with statues cornering their rooms, contrast with the top floor Alberghettino prison where the monk Savonarola was tortured. Savonarola drew attention to the corruption of the pope Adrian VI, a Borgia, and tried to dislodge the Medicis' grip on Florence. At first he was acclaimed by the Florentines but they turned against him after his bonfires of vanities, when nude paintings, cosmetics and jewellery were burnt and indecent dress and gambling attacked. Built between 1298–1314, the palace got its name (meaning 'old') when the Medicis moved in 1550 to the Pitti Palace. The loggia was built in the 14th century with arches and two rows of statues. Alongside is the soaring 94 metre (308 foot) Arnulphs tower, which is lit up by oil lamps on special occasions. It is topped by a lily, the city symbol. Its bell, known as 'the cow', once summoned the citizens to the town's defence.

In front of the Palazzo Vecchio is the Neptune fountain, known as the 'big white man' and by this is a marble slab marking the spot where Savonarola was hanged and burned in 1498. Among the famous statues near the palace entrance is the Marzocco, a heraldic lion symbol. It is joined once a year by other live animals, when the city offers free oats to all donkeys, horses and mules brought to the piazza.

Florence was originally an outpost in the valley below the hill

top, which is now Fiesole and was then an Etruscan hill fort. Later the Romans came and made Florence a military camp, which they called Florentia.

The importance of the whole site lay in the narrow shallow area of the **river Arno** (above); the only place where it could be crossed. Flat-bottomed boats were used at first but the Etruscans created the original bridge on the site of the present Ponte Vecchio (second from bottom of picture), the only one still existing from the Middle Ages, surviving the German destruction in World War II and standing up to the tremendous and

destructive flooding in November 1966. This flood ruined a thousand paintings in the city, destroyed Cimabue's *Crucifixion*, ruined the Santa Croce church and submerged a million books in the Florentine National library. Santa Croce is particularly loved by Florentines; it is where Galileo and Machiavelli are buried and contains frescoes painted by Giotto.

The bridging point of the Arno gave Florence the key to guarding the north-south trade of Italy and the city swiftly became a commercial leader. Its currency, stamped with a lily, was strong and reliable. Florence founded international banking and commercial insurance and with the backing of these riches gave the world the great arts of the Renaissance. The Ponte Vecchio still reflects artistic wealth in its little row of shops, some devoted to souvenirs, others to superb leatherwork (the Leather School is in the monastery of Santa Croce), shoes, delicately engraved silver, mosaics, and gold work. Across the top of the shops on the bridge can be seen the remains of the half-mile long, enclosed corridor Cosimo de Medici built to link his offices in the Uffizi Palace with his home, the Pitti Palace.

Venice

The high street of Venice is a 5 metre (17 foot) deep, **S-shaped canal** (above) running 4 kilometres (2½ miles) through the heart of the city from the Piazzale Roma to St Mark's. Originally it was a branch of a river running out into the lagoon. The Vaporetti (water buses) numbers 1 and 2 run the length of the Grand Canal and over to the Lido, the bathing resort area. It takes about an hour and is a popular trip, for it gives the whole panorama of Venice in one ride. Motor-boats are quicker as they take a short cut.

The Grand Canal's banks are topped with 200 palaces built from the 12th to 18th centuries in a variety of styles. Obelisks atop building façades were granted to captains who did well in the service of the Serenissima republic. The Grand Canal was always an attraction for visitors especially the artistic; Byron swam in it, Wagner wrote Tristan and Isolde alongside it, Henry James, A. E. Housman, Ruskin, Goethe, Hemingway, Mark Twain and Churchill all stayed by it; Browning died overlooking it. He had an apartment in the Ca' Rezzonico. The Palazzo Rezzonico now sums up the gaiety and decadence of eighteenth century Venice. In the ballroom are trompe l'oeil effects and the top floor of the palace is a baroque museum with a complete pharmacy of the period. The Palazzo Pesaro contains modern art, as does Peggy Guggenheim's Vernei dei Leoni.

Until motor boats appeared in 1881, gondolas provided Venice's only transport system. Numbers have dropped from about 20,000 in the 16th century to around 470 today. However, gondolas are still used for the *traghetti*, the ferry crossing of the main canals to save long walks and for private trips which are more expensive and need subtle bargaining. Weddings call for decorated gondolas, and for funerals, gondolas carrying the coffins move solemnly out to the cemetery island of San Michele, where tombs are constructed in the style of a filing cabinet to save land space.

It takes three years to learn to become a gondolier and don the familiar straw hat, black trousers and striped or plain shirt. A man called a ganzer helps gondolas to moor; hooking them in with a candy striped pole. Gondoliers are skilled at negotiating the sharp dark corners of back canals, shouting, instead of using a horn (a peaceful plus of Venice), and avoiding barges laden with vegetables or furniture, the pantechnicons of Venice. There is only one traffic light in Venice, and the official speed limit is 5 km (3 miles) per hour on city canals.

The Grand Canal widens out towards the lagoon by St Mark's and the little piazzetta with its marble lions, which provides a look-out point towards the island of San Giorgio Maggiore. Two granite columns remain by the waterside, one topped by St Theodore, the other by the winged lion symbol of Venice; locals think it portends death to walk between them, as executions were once held here.

St Mark's Square (right) is the only large square in Venice. Napoleon once called it the drawing room of Europe. On a summer Sunday morning up to 40,000 visitors and locals pass through, to listen to the lively bands which compete by the pavement cafés and small old coffee shops like Florian's and Quadri, and to feed the swirling pigeons. A recent pigeon clean-up campaign by means of netting and the Pill was reversed by bird lovers. In winter, the square is quiet and misted, duck-boards making paths when the high waters come. The square was originally a convent garden and slopes towards the church, which is faced with four bronze Greek horses dating from 400–200 B.C. Doges (Venetian dukes) were crowned and buried in the original St Mark's, which was their chapel. The present building dates from 1063–1094. It has one large and five small domes in the form of a Greek cross, which are lavishly decorated with gilded mosaics designed by Titian, Veronese, Tintoretto and Bassano. The church is said to contain the body of St Mark, stolen from Alexandria by Venetian merchants, who hid it from Moslem discovery under a pile of pork.

In the square, the campanile, after existing for 1,000 years, fell down in 1902. By 1912 an exact replica had been built, all 99 metres (324 feet) of it, a good height for

city views and where Galileo showed a doge his new telescope. The British Venice in Peril fund has restored the 16th century loggetta which serves as its entrance. Marks on the tower base show the height of the 1966 flood waters. In the Middle Ages, misbehaved clergy were hung in cages from the top of the campanile.

The Doge's Palace (right, above and below) summed up the immense maritime wealth and power of Venice. Alongside its giant staircase inside are massive statues of Neptune and Mars representing sea and land power. The rooms from which Venice was ruled can be seen as they were 400 years ago. Though looted by Napoleon, paintings by Tintoretto and Veronese remain: Veronese in the Council of Ten, where punishments were meted out; Tintoretto in the Great Council Chamber (shown in the picture), where early in the democratic ages of Venice the citizens elected the doge (later only the nobles were allowed to). Here in 1797 the last doge abdicated and Venice fell to Napoleon. Behind the doge's throne in this great ornate room is Tintoretto's painting of *Paradise*, the largest oil painting in the world.

Portraits of 76 doges line the cornice below the ceiling here. One has a black curtain across it and a note that the 14th century doge, Marin Faliero, was executed for treason. Faliero's main crime was to try to exert some influence on events. For the doges, though they were proud captains at sea, were little more than pampered prisoners, without real power on land. In the 7th century the lagoon communities were ruled by military commanders, a dux or doge, carrying out the orders of the Byzantine empire. In 774, the leaders moved to a fortress, now the Arsenal. By the end of the 13th century, the doges' power had been curbed. They were no longer a monarchy but were left to police an autocratic council of ten, then a council of 1,000 nobles. From 1310 to 1797, when the Venetian republic ended, no major constitutional changes were made.

The Doge's Palace was built in the 9th century and restored after fires in the 14th century. The 15th century entrance, the Porta della Carta (paper gate), had the council's decrees nailed on it; and a stone lion mouth was the receptacle for secret information and criticisms. The doges in death were magnificent to the last, if somewhat gruesome in taste, as can be seen in tombs of the church of St Peter and Paul (San Zanipolo to Venetians).

Boats link islands in the Venetian lagoon. It is a mysterious area, where, in winter, fog bells boom eerily along the pallio, the rows of wooden posts guiding the boats through the channels. Burano island has changed little over the years. Its bell tower tilts to rival Pisa's leaning tower and its San Martino church contains a Calvary by Tiepolo. But its main attraction, earning it the nickname of 'Venetian Montparnasse' and the affection of painters is the colour-washed housing that edges the canals: pink, yellow, ochre and russet. It's the way the Buranelli keep up with the Joneses. Burano is a fishing island; the boats nose their way to the owner's back door along little canals and are tied up there. Men sit outside houses mending nets, while their women make the fine pillow lace for which the island is famed and which is kept alive with a small lace school.

Other islands include San Francesco del Deserto, said to have been visited by St Francis, where those escaping modern life can stay in the monastery for a while. Then there is Torcello with its haunted air, due to a decline in its

population from 20,000 to under 100. An empty marble 'emperor's' chair stands outside the cathedral, where rising damp has reached the ceiling mosaics, as it also has in the Santa Fosca church next door. Ruskin called Torcello 'the mother of Venice' and Venetians come here to celebrate wedding anniversaries, with blessings in the church, followed by a meal at the Locanda Cipriani, a sister establishment to the famous Harry's Bar near St Mark's.

Murano has been the glass-making island since 1292. Now rather crude animals are quickly fashioned for visitors, but the glass museum shows off Venetian glass arts since Roman days. Mirrors were a Venetian speciality; the area invented eye glasses, made the best windows in Europe but declined when its crystal secrets became more widely known.

Bridges, as well as gondolas, were vital needs of this

city built on water. There are about 450 bridges, 50 of which were privately built to enable owners to get to their palaces. The most sombre is the Bridge of Sighs, a double corridored bridge connecting the Doge's Palace with the prisons, where Casanova was once held. It was said the condemned sighed as they caught a final brief glimpse of the outside world through the fretted windows in the sides.

The Rialto is the pioneer bridge; in fact early Venice was called the town of Rialto (meaning 'high bank'). Shakespeare's *Merchant of Venice* contains many references to merchants in the Rialto, then the hub of commercial life and it is still the Piccadilly Circus of Venice. The banks around the Rialto are one of the few walking areas. Demonstrations, an essential part of Italian political life, are held there; Casanova talks of 18th century

beaux and their ladies walking there in the early hours
after a party; and the statue of Goldoni, the 18th century
writer who created 120 comedies, keeps watch with pigeons
perched on his tricorn hat. Cafés are laid out along
the banks below the bridge and tables are at a premium.
Behind the bridge are the city's fish and vegetable markets
established since 1097, where the products are particularly
fresh and good.

The present **Rialto bridge** (above) succeeded various wooden
bridges. It was opened in 1592 built on 6,000 wooden piles to a
design by Antonio da Ponte, who beat rivals like Michelangelo
and Palladio to get the contract. Until 1854 the Rialto was the
vital east-west Venice connection and the only bridge spanning
the Grand Canal.

Venice is a beautiful city, which has always attracted
artists, who sit on its waterfronts to capture the limpid
lights of the **canals** (right) on their canvas. For other
visitors, the romance of the city can be experienced in a
gondola. Probably Turkish in origin, **the gondola** (far
right) is a lopsided, high-prowed, virtually uncapsizable
boat. They assumed their present shape in the 15th
century. Weighing 590 kilogrammes (1300 lb), they are
made by hand with 280 pieces of wood and have traditional
walnut blocks for the oar rest and a bronze sea horse on
the prow.

INDEX
(Figures in italics refer to illustrations)

Alberobello 26, *26*
Amalfi 28; cathedral 47, *47*
Aosta 10
Arno, River 56, *56–7*
Assisi cathedral 47, *47*
Asti 18, 35

Barcaccia fountain, Rome 54
Barumini 44
Beqizzole castle *23*, 24
Bernini, Giovanni 43, 47, 50
Bernini, Pietro 54
Boboli gardens, Florence 56
Bologna 10, 13, 14–16; carnival 35
Bolzano 13
Bordighera 18
Borromean islands 10, 12
Botticelli, Sandro 44–5
Bridge of Sighs, Venice 61
Burano 60

Cagliari 24
Calabria 22, 29, 35
Camogli 13
Caprera 25
Capri *24–5*, *25–6*
Castel Mola 24
Castel Sant'Angelo, Rome *50*, 51
Cattolica 19
Cefalu *20–21*, 22
Cheeses, Italian 33
Chiavari 13
Cimabue, Giovanni 42, 47, 57
Cirella 29
Coliseum, Rome *40–41*, 42
Como, Lake 10, 38
Cortina d'Ampezzo 13
Cosenza 35
Courmayeur 10
Cristallo, Monte 13
Crotone 35

Dante Alighieri 15, 19, 44
Da Vinci, Leonardo 44, 45
Diamante 29
Dino, Isola di 29
Doge's Palace, Venice 60, *60*, *61*
Dolomite mountains *11*, 12–13

Etna, Mount 22, *22*, 24

Fiesole 56
Florence 32, 35, 38, 50, 54–7

Garda, Lake 12
Giotto 42, 47, 57; bell tower 54
Gondolas and gondoliers 58, 62, *63*

Hanbury gardens (Capo Mortola) 18–19
Herculaneum 29, 43

Isola Bella 10, *10*
Isola Madre 12

Jesolo, Lido di 19

Lipari 22
Lugano, Lake 10

Maggiore, Lake 10, 12
Matera 26, *27*, 28
Merano 13
Michelangelo 44, 45, 47, 54, 56
Milan 13–14, *14*; cathedral 10, 14
Moneglia 19, *19*
Monferrato hills 18, *18*
Mosaics 42, 43, 44
Murano 60

Naples 29, *29*, 33, 35
Nuraghe buildings, Sardinia *43*, 43–4

Paestum 42, *42*
Palazzo Vecchio, Florence 50, 56
Paraggi 13
Pisa *4–5*
Pitti Palace, Florence 54, *55*, 56
Pizza, types of 35, *35*
Pompeii 29, 43, *43*, 44
Ponte Vecchio, Florence 56, 57
Pont St Martin *8–9*, 10
Portofino *12*, 13
Positano 28
Praia a Mare 29

Railways, Italian 32
Rapallo 13
Ravello 28
Ravenna, churches of 42, 44, *44*
Rezzonico, Palazzo (Venice) 58
Rialto Bridge, Venice 61, 62, *62*
Riccione 19
Rimini 19
Rome *49*, 50–4; Via Veneto 35

St Francis of Assisi 47, 60
St Mark's Square, Venice 58, *59*
St Peter's, Rome 45, *46*, 47, *52–3*, 54
San Francesco del Deserto 60
San Fruttuoso 13
San Gimignano 15
San Marino *16*, 16–17
San Petronio, Bologna 16
San Remo 18
Santa Croce, Florence 57
Santa Lucia 29, 35
Santa Margherita 13
Sardinia 22, 24; nuraghe buildings *43*, 43–4
Savonarola, Girolamo 44–5, 56
Scalea 29, *29*
Sforza castle, Milan 44, 47
Sicily 22–4
Signoria, Piazza della (Florence) 35, 54, *55*, 56
Silk industry, Italian 10, 38
Sistine Chapel, Rome 44, 45, 54
Solda 13
Sorrento 28, *28*

Spanish Steps, Rome 51, *51*
Stromboli 22

Taormina 24, 35
Taranto 35
Tomatoes, Italian 38, *38*
Torcello 60
Torre del Lago 19
Trevi fountain, Rome *48–49*, 50–1
Trulli dwellings, Apulia 26
Tuscany *6–7*, 38

Uffizi Gallery, Florence 44, 57

Vatican 54; museum 54
Venice *2–3*, 50, 58–62; Lido 19; regattas 35, *36–37*
Verona 14; amphitheatre 14, *15*
Vesuvius, Mount 22, 25, 29, 43
Vulcano 22

Wines, Italian 13, 18

ACKNOWLEDGEMENTS

The publishers wish to thank the following organizations and individuals for their kind permission to reproduce the photographs in this book:

William Albert Allard/Image Bank 37; Audio Impact/Stephen Benson 40–41, 52–53, 61 inset; A. Boccaccio/Image Bank 48–49; Didier Dorval/Image Bank 58; Gregory Evans 24–25, 28, 46, 51, 59; Peter Frey/Image Bank 14; Larry Dale Gordon/Image Bank 54; Gucci, London 32 above; Robert Harding Associates 33, 39; Francisco Hidalgo/Image Bank 2–3, 60–61; Image Bank 22; Italian State Tourist Board 45 above; Bullaty Lomeo/Image Bank 6–7, 47 left, 50; Nino Mascardi/Image Bank 26–27; Steve Niedorf/Image Bank 63; M. Pedone/Image Bank 8–9, 10, 15 above, 16–17, 18–19, 20–21, 26 left, 29 left, 47 right, 55 above; Pictor International 12–13, 32 below, 62 below; Guido Alberto Rossi/Image Bank 23, 35, 43 below; Scala 45 below; Eric Schweikardt/Image Bank 4–5; Spectrum Colour Library 11, 15 below, 30–31, 44, 62 above; John Lewis Stage/Image Bank 42; R. Stradtmann 1; Amadeo Vergani/Image Bank 29 right, 34, 38, 43 above, 56–57; Zefa/G. Barone 19 above, 55 below.